Rain

CW00409494

heartache, life, and emotions

by S J Williams

———————

To my family.

Sad poems can make you smile.
Happy poems can make you cry.
Emotions are subjective.

I'm ok.

—

Rainclouds

A collection of poems from experience, imagination, and the world around us.

heartache, life, and emotions

Rainclouds

In innocence the clouds collide
In retrospect we should have cried.
Taken by the sudden storm
Heart beats faster, we were warned
That in a fragile, tempted world
Strangers walk where we were scorned
An age ago when we were kings
Chances and changes bring newer things
Twisted by fate and circumstances
We made our beds
Took our chances
Some things played out. Not many.
Do you think it's funny?
Walking every steeping slope
Would bring a lack of lifetime hope?
Is this vision playing out from youth?
Where did you envisage the journey to go?
It's not here.
Here can be rearranged from today
Despite the words that folk may say.
Today is precious
Today is kind
Kinder than what you had in mind.
When clouds collide, it makes no sound
Tears on cheeks are not allowed
So, look to rain clouds
When worlds collide
Stare and see them passing by.

Is This What You Said?

Have we run out of things to talk about?
Glum faces, no eyes making contact.
Do you want out?
What shall we say when we get back?
Just brush our teeth and hit the sack?
You yawn and drink, no interest in me
Who did you expect me to be?
Who did I want you to become?
Who were we when this had begun?
What changed?
Or did we just stay the same?
Grew stale in our familiarity?
Became too used to us as family?
Do we wish upon a past?
A past we vowed to see us last
Have we run out of things to say?
How can we look forward to today
If no reason springs to mind to stay.
Perhaps we leave that past behind.
I won't mind.
Now drink up. I'm tired.
Let's go to bed
And hold each other silently instead.

The Words I Said

I said words
Didn't mean them
I tried hard
Don't believe them
Take my truth, twist it as you see fit
Look me in the eye, believe it
Shake it up, this life is shit
Regret, don't make me reveal it
Walking away, this truth is lies
Lying on my back - starry skies
This truth spreads like wildfire
Alive, but see me as a liar
I'm a tryer.
Desire, functioning as a winner
Set me down, feed me dinner.
Fed up, winning on life
Cut me up, swipe the knife.
Believe again, not my word
Don't believe the words you heard
I called it
This is it- I regret
But life for me ain't over yet
Bet your hand
Deal again.
Take a chance on this.
Stand.
Hold my hand.

I said words I may deny
I would cry
Shamed by the man as I stood by.
I said words
You said nothing
This moment in my life counts for zero
Never stood here as a hero
Took each step, day by day
Don't want this pain to go away
I stray
Religion taught me how to pray
Faith has made me see this way.
I said words
I'm not proud.
I said words
Voices - too loud
Telling me to change the script
I changed a bit
My mind still lives the same
Again, I recall it.
When I said words, I regret.
I'm sorry.
Please forget the words I said.

A Penny For Your Year

Be grateful for the last year, you never needed
more
Nothing to expect than what came the day before
Put a penny on your doorstep on the night of New
Year's Eve
And if it stays there overnight
Then this year you'll receive
Hope, health, and happiness for the year ahead
And if it's gone, you've blessed this wish
To someone else instead.

Sunset Boulevard

A cold and lonely night on Sunset Boulevard
Wandering like a nomad
For this life, I am glad.
Shopping cart full of useless lies
Sleeping in and out under unforgiving skies.
A cold and shameful day on Temple Way
Wondering what made me so mad
Tonight, I'm feeling bad
Shopping trolley full of memories
On the street, many enemies.
Worlds apart, the same old tale
How did I lose, how did I fail?

Where to go to gain back my pride?
Who is there? My faith subsides.
Sunset Boulevard was in my dreams
No in between.
This life may never be the way it seems.
But sunsets fade and create new dawns
I wake to hope.
My anger torn.
Here I wake, a brand-new day
Sunset Boulevard, so far away
Rich or poor, sad, or elated
This life is what I made,
Created.

Distant

Distant beats resounding in my heart
Thumping tunes, beating memories start.
Aggravated hearts and me.
Distant.
How were we supposed to be?
Were we close? Did we fight?
Where do we sleep tomorrow night?
Sleepless nights, longer days.
These dreams
Shattered by reality
It's just a phase
And as dreams fade
We see the endless ways
I convinced you to stay
Step closer, breathe
Please don't go astray.
Be closer than you were today.

The Light Tomorrow

The light on the horizon lowers
I turn to brothers...
Still the darkness follows
Tomorrow stumbles
I fell again, too many troubles
Intensity of emotion doubles
Struggles - too many nights alone
It's not my home, but I am here.
How did this transpire?
Fire dampened, but flames grow higher.
The light fades faster, bursting bubbles
As I fall, hold my hand
I understand it all.
It's not my place to criticise
Eyes wide
The light on the horizon fades
Walking blind throughout these days.
Somewhere shines a new horizon
I'm alive and the prize - I have eyes on
Count to ten, start again.
The light tomorrow will always fade
Dreams of promises we made
I turn to brothers
But darkness remains
We'll never be the same again.

Younger

I was just a hanger-on
My friendship bones were not that strong
Despite the laughs
The memories
The time
At some point further down the line
An expanse between my memory,
Reality, and what I wanted it to be,
—Would be the vast emptiness
That stole my childhood faithfulness.
Did I ever count?
I was in, but for so long now I'm out.
Younger years to me were bliss
That's the feeling I miss.

Twisted Logic

Contribution to retribution
Self-punished for a revelation
This muted station belongs to a nation
Smile, you're on camera.
When the world knows your name
No longer anonymous
We become one of us.
Smiling never brought us down
Crows and frowns
Drinking whisky and circus clowns
The past doesn't haunt, it praises
Edible mice, words on pages
Make a dollar from the words
I'm alone, how did we get here?
Fear?
Steering towards the strange…
Rearrange the thought.
Is this the feeling I sought?
Edible mice… is that a thing?
It's quiet now
Make the phone ring...

This Moment

Fucked up thinking.
Went to bed, dreams awry
Woke to horror of reality
The future verse has made me cry.
Who are we? Where do we belong?
Was it so right to see this injustice all along.
Do we stay strong?
Where does strength play a part?
When has greed already torn your heart?
This politics, this injustice
It must make blood boil
Your millions don't count for shit
You pay them to supply the oil
Corruption comes in many guises
Your political surprises
They keep you numb
Where do we go, how did we come from here?
I voted. But not for this
I made my word heard, my reminiscent pledge.
Contribution to society stripped.
Let the wankers play their game
But tonight, I'll never sleep the same.
The scary movie faded. Reality hit.
Shit, it's just the same.

A Brighter Me

Tomorrow took away my future
Spurned by the actions of today
Yesterday fed negative passion
That stood before me, blocked the way.
Knocking down this emotion
Overcoming each (and every) trial
May take more time
Will steal my life
And make me stumble for a while
But in the dim and distant view
Brighter suns will shine anew
Thinking this is all there is
Is seeing all that was
This deeper strength will grow so strong
A brighter me, and never us.

The Darkness of My Tormented Dream

I may have to leave
Agnostic thoughts
A distant breeze.
Strangled by forgiving dreams
Lonely strangers, then me.
Sharing wonders
Seeing days
Amazed by simple, trusting ways.
Writing poetry by sight.
Goodnight.
What do we see?
Darkness of infinite minds
The future dims - it reminds me;
Who did we leave behind?
Rewind. Reverse. Write a different verse
Light follows the night
Together we will be alright
Unforgiving sight of mind
Seeking, relentlessly
Fighting thoughtlessly,
Are my images alright?
Go to bed and count to ten.
Tomorrow we shall start again.

Who Are You? Why Am I?

You'll never define me
Search - you'll never find me
You'll never undermine me
Even though the past behind me
Has led me to this moment
I won't be boxed or put away
Too many paths have crossed this way
Too many me, which one is true?
One day I'm happy, next I'm blue
Today for me, tomorrow you.
Sensible and senseless, all rolled in to one
Incoherent yesterday, today a poet, father, son.
Words of salvation, followed by damnation
Follower of faith and beauty
Now turned ugly, feeling dirty
One day sober, next day gone
But I knew this double me all along
One day sky blue, next day red
One day feels alive, the next day
Dead in inside, too much to hide
Too much grief and too much pain
But wake anew and start again.
You'll never define me
Search inside, I never found me
Don't try to understand me
Stand beside, don't walk behind me.

Meet Me Tomorrow

Meet me at the corner of yesterday
Let's go back to how we were.
We'll dance again, share a dream
Forget the future, and in between.
Meet me how you knew me
Nothing changed but life.
As age becomes a changing face
The places change, but not the race.
Meet me on a Sunday
Calm and restful, sunshine warm
Sunday papers, coffee cups
Embracing downs, enjoying ups.
Meet me after years of hurt
See the way I changed
This broken soul, tired of pain
Tomorrow's come, never change again.

Too Many Dreams

Too many dreams
Too many tomorrows to say goodbye to
Faith and hope collided
My reality of life subsided
As I said goodbye to the truth
Unguided by expression
Untruthful to the past I tread
This future life I dread
I said it would never happen to me
I was blinded
Short sighted
I still sleep restlessly, unguided
Flying solo, I tried it
Not for me.
I fail.
I walked on every broken trail
I stood there thinking
Eyes blinking
But life has made this body frail
Give up the drinking, but it feels less real
Don't you understand the way I feel?
I'm broken, can you fix me?
Pass me by or trick me.
Too many dreams, shattered at once
On the edge of life, I stand.
Fading hopes.
Lonely nights, drifting sand.

Little Lost Louis

The game was simple -
Keep the child by your side
But Louis slipped his reigns off
In Cornwall toilets he would hide
I lose.
I lost loose Louis in Looe's loos.
When found, Louis cried.

Unreasonable

Filter the past
Embrace that which served you well
Discard the trash
Face each day with brighter eyes
Hold on to truth
Ignore the lies
Live each day as new and inspiring
Put yourself in the mix
There's no joy in hiding
From the glories that this earth has in store
Wake me up
I want more.
Each new step brings memories new
Each new day has hope for you.

Lay upon the grass at night
Stare skyward to the heaven
These moments, precious
I'm alright.
Take the future in your soul
Grasp the beauty tonight.
Forgive me, forget me
I really don't care
I wish I never saw you standing there.
I've filtered my past to see you gone
I now know where I am
Where I belong.
There's a new future
Where happiness and laughter reign
You'll never see me cry again.

Lemons

We took lemons and gave them bread
Stole some sugar,
Danced in streets of golden thread
Played our part
Conceived a dream on what they said
Sticking to the rules we read
We stole their future
Left them dead.
Trigger fingers, red and raw
Not ashamed of the things we saw
We bled
{They said we'd bleed}
Too many broken hearts conceived
Destruction played on every ground
Ashamed of this, we found
A common land on which we stood
Was this for war or was it for good?
We took their life and gave them hell
Too late to back down now,
Too late to stand against this machine
That made our hearts so cold and mean
Give me back the life I knew
We took too much, we cried too.
Take me home, this is not the end
Future fades.
I am your friend.

Hey

Hey, how are you?
Did sunlight fill your life?
Or are you like the rest of us
Where life cuts like a knife?
Hey, how are you?
Did you find it tough like me?
Or are you sailing silently
Across the life you see?
Somewhere beyond the horizon
A future glimmers bright
So, hold my hand and let's be close
If only for tonight.
Hey, where are you?
Did darkness fill your day?
Or are you just ignoring me
What should I do or say?
Somewhere beyond the horizon
A future glimmers bright
So hold my hand and let's be close
If only for tonight.
If only you believed me
If only we could dream
If only life was plain and simple
If only, I'm lonely.
Hey, where are you?
Did I not say that I would call?
The darkness left so suddenly

We could have had it all.
Somewhere beyond the horizon
A future glimmers bright
So, hold my and let's be close
If only for tonight.

Smile

All I wanted was a smile
To see your face illuminate a while
To see you dance among the strangers
Memories of my life..
The joys
The dangers
I dreamt of your breath
Your touch, your words
What life is left?
Stay a while
Smile
It's all I need.

Absence Of Magic

Twas the night before Christmas when all thro' the
house
The only sound heard was the click of a mouse.
The stockings were raided, no walnut in sight
But hopes for St Nick were still set alight.
The children were playing, a game of Fortnite
With visions of internet stardom in sight.
And mother in jeans, vodka in hand
Would sleep well tonight wherever she lands.
When out on the lawn there arose such a clatter
Dad was home late, somewhat drunken, and fatter.
Away to the window I flew like a flash
To see my old man stumble, fall into the trash
The moon on the breast of the new fallen snow
Confused my old man, gave him nowhere to go.
'Cause a midnight shot, and eight pints of beer
Saw my dad come in gingerly, bended by ear
In a moment I knew, I just had to retreat
More rapid than angels, as he lost his feet
And he shouted, and swore, with hate in his eyes
This story is common, it's no great surprise.
"Now bedtime, now sleep, now just go away!"
"You're clumsy, you're stupid, get out of my way!"
"Just go away, go away, go away all"
"I'm going to stumble, I'm going to fall"
As dry wine before a man who has failed
When they meet with an obstacle, they will be
derailed.

So up to bed now, this cold Christmas night
Forgotten the toys, no presents in sight.
And then in a twinkling, I heard from above
A pawing, a struggle, no sign of love.
As I hid under covers, awaiting the scream
Nobody came to my side it would seem.
The man who then entered, all dressed in not much
Would hold out his hand and offer a touch
No bundle of toys were slung on his back
He looked like my father but different in fact
His eyes - they were different, no twinkle was there
His gaze was now evil, I shrank at his stare.
His droll little mouth, was static and mute
And the beard on his chin made him look like a
brute
The fag in his mouth was held tight by his teeth
And the smoke, it encircled his head like a wreath
He had a bold head, and a horrible smell
That reeked of disgust I remember too well
He was chubby and plump, a horrible man
And I cry when I think how anyone can
Be evil at Christmas, and then somehow steal
My childhood dreams; and now make me feel
That something is missing. Something's not right.
But to all, Happy Christmas, but for me it's
goodnight.

Severance

Severance and deliverance
Strive to keep alive
Happiness of fortitude
Regret, I'll take the other side.
Summer's glare, were you there?
Standing still and hopeless.
The most we enjoyed was lust
Who did we trust?
Us?
Forever seeking truth,
Ending in forgotten dreams
Life is never what it seems
The extremes of ill forgotten belief
Stand upon the lonely street
Hide your thoughts.
Sit down, shut up
Isn't being here enough?
It's tough, but is this life alive?
Where did we go
Who were we with, and who tried?
Who cried?
Which of us kept the faith alive?
And still the feelings deep inside
Hurt so much, I want to hide.
Where do we go now?
Who do we look to to trust?
Gaining speed, this memory fades

Faking life, again and again
Each waking day sees a different self
Don't leave me here
Take a look and stay with me
And God forbid you be yourself.
The sheets were cold, but the bed was made
Yesterday saw trinkets of who we saved
Lying lifeless, now I see
The future of who I was born to be
Creating passions out of dust
Drawing images of us
If you ever felt the same
If we ever lived this life again
Then hold me closer than you did
Preach to me stronger
Teach me for longer
I was never a soldier
A wanderer in this infinite cycle
A warrior, unfashionable by demand
Every time I reach for sand
It trickles through my clutching hand.

Terracotta Stars

I'm so afraid of being me
These terracotta stars I see
Don't shine so bright
These terracotta stars are dim
My story fades, where do I start?
Where do I begin?
Stars should shine
Bright and blue
I was waiting, where were you?
I'm so afraid of being me
These terracotta stars I see
Don't shine at all
But the beauty of them
Still enthrals my passion
Where do I begin?
Stars should shimmer
Me and you
I'm still waiting. Who are you?
I'm so afraid of telling lies
These terracotta stars are wise
Don't shine today
They tell a story, oh so loud
Stare skyward
Who is proud?
Stars fade
Dark and grey
Thoughts of you, they fade away

I'm so afraid of showing up
When everyone asks me how I cope
Nothing shines
These terracotta stars are calling
My story ends
Where is the beginning?

Christabel

Christabel sits on the bottom step
Black and bruised from the pain she felt
Wondering why this happened to her
Scared to move, she waits
Daddy has been gone too long
Daddy is so big and strong
He keeps me safe, she thinks
Daddy wakes each day and drinks
He drinks for all the errors made
He drinks for all the games he played
And Christabel sits on the bottom step
Waiting for daddy's loving breath

I saw you again.

I'm scared of how I feel
Ashamed this life I lead is real
So sorry for the hurt I cause
The curtain's down, there's no applause
And as the sunset turns to night
The comfort comes that I'm alright
Is shattered by the very thought
This speckled life is what I fought
But somewhere in my distant past
A love ignites that's built to last
Future's grey but hope shines bright
So, make my past shine bright tonight
You sat there, smiling, beauty true
I forgot the love I saw in you
I see it now, flame reignited
Feelings churn, so excited
Stay, be here and hold me tight
Even if you stay the night
I'll feel again, I'll feel anew
The feelings that I held for you.

The Jungle Held A Meeting

The jungle held a meeting
Who was who and who they're eating
Lion took a slow walk to the stage
"I am the king, the God, the mage"
Then crocodile, he made a stand
"You may be great, but just on land"
"I'm the greatest river foe"
"The river, you will never go"
"Fair enough" the lion stated
The crowd fell silent and then they waited.
"Excuse me", came the eagle's boast
"The sky is where I rule the most"
"I see my prey from in the air"
"Rivers, land, I find it there"
And meanwhile all the other beast
Were scared on what these three would feast.
Then from the back, a voice aloud
Came shrilling through the wild crowd
"I am human, I trump you all"
"I have weapons, I'll watch you fall"
"I'll desolate your living space"
"Pollute your air, remove your race"
"How dare you?" called the smallest bee
"Why can't you understand how we"
"Are not complaining of our demise"
"From land or river or from the skies"
"We live and die as God intended"

"We help you humans live so splendid"
"If you kill us, you will not survive"
"So try your best to keep us alive!"
"But you kill, and eat each other!"
The human said without a shudder.
The bee called out without delay
"Just hear me now to what I say…"
"Although this meeting has been called"
"We came together, despite who ruled"
"We know we all may live or die"
"But nature makes that call, not I"
"Mankind is calling all the shots"
"Our natural word is fading lots"
And from amidst the gathered crowd
A lonely voice, so humbly loud
"I am orangutang"
"You humans kill, you selfish man"
"I walk this world now, so alone"
"I've lost my friends; I've lost my home"
The human stood there, looked, and cried
He felt the hurt he'd caused inside
"I'll make this mess undone."
"Too late", said bee
"It has begun"

I don't want to lose you again.

Can we just be friends?
Look at where this future ends?
Are we alright to just forget
Is this life a solemn bet?
Relive the past and start again
Entrust our feelings, make amends?
Go tonight and hold my dream
Of you and me, what will that mean?
Do you feel the same way too?
Do you see a me and you?
Every night will pass so slow
Now I'll never let you go.

Not Today

Where do you go to when the world turns grey?
Who told you it would be better today?
When you woke, who said today was just a joke?
Who put you down when you arose?
Whose future stood before you, who's words
were those?
Not mine
They were yours
And everything you hear rings true.
So, whenever you are feeling blue
Deny the voice that rings inside
Hold your head up, have some pride.
You're better than you were today
The sadness - it may not go away
But every breath you take
From this day forward
Life will say
You are amazing
You are unique
If life hits hard
Turn your cheek
If life presents a life of grey
Then make a stand, say "not today "

Our Love Aligns

Playing games as children when our parents
were away
Climbing on the haystacks, you and me.
My fantasy of you as gorgeous as you were
As beautiful as you are.
Tomorrow when I wake
I will not fear the sounds or sights
Of those who saw
Of those who have never seen
Those who never had the love we had
Find the journey
Discover and find the path we took
To those who never travelled, look…
I look into your eyes and pray
That you and I will be one
Despite our thoughts on east and west
Society would never know
Hold my soul, hold my heart
Our love aligns so beautiful
We do not see the pain
We see us, together.

This life

This life grows weaker as I age
I've painted words on every page
I've viewed the pleasure and the past
Taken chances while they last
I saw the trouble as it grew
Loved a little, trusted few
I danced on streets with pure emotion
Caused a stir, a youth devotion.
Played my part, sang the song
And now I know it won't be long
Before I take my final bow
Upon this stage I loved somehow
A singing swan, a last regret
A final chance, a final bet
This life is full of great surprises
One day low, the next it rises
Today I save my final breath
I'll give until there's no life left
And yet I know I'll carry on
I know my heart, it's still as strong
This life grows stronger now I see
Love divides both you and me.
So, leave me here, I'll be fine
You know you broke this heart of mine
I'll wake up soon and see the day
Hope for better, hope and pray
I painted words on every page
And life goes on as I age.

Don't Judge Me

Don't judge me
I lost my faith in humanity
We see the pain
Of life's insanity
You see it too, too quiet to say
Your anger will show it's face one day
You'll question life
Just as I did too
You'll find a faith in something new
Yet deep inside
The questions rise
And it will come as no surprise
That answers, they are hard to find
As you try, leave tears behind
Don't judge me
I am just like you
I'm on the search for something new
A path that leads to brighter days
A clarity beyond the haze
I found my faith
It keeps me strong
Hold my hand and come along
I'll take you down this path of hope
With knowledge, wisdom, how to cope
Don't judge me
I found my faith in something new
You can be here and feel it too

It takes a leap
It takes a change
It may feel odd
It may feel strange
Don't judge me for how I feel
Or why I try to make this real
Hold my hand and hear my heart
Tomorrow sees a brand-new start.

We Had Fun

I held your hand, a setting sun.
I did my best, and we had fun
On that night when everything changed
Everything lost was rearranged
And we both felt the same
Something different, something strange.
Feelings started to erupt
This was all just so abrupt.
We both knew what was meant to be
It only happens when you see
How we were then, but this is now
It's happened but we don't know how.

The Sun

As daylight shimmers on open fields
I awake to birds, singing glorious melodies
Fresh new dawn brings fresh new hope
Skies illuminate
As darkness sets across the land
I stumble. singing tunes of failure
Slumber of a tireless future
Skies darken.

Winter comes.

Broken wood, twigs, and walks
Sometimes silent, someone talks
Dogs are barking, running free
Hand in hand you walk with me
Winter sun and morning dew
Walking as the sun breaks through
Morning coffee, scruffy hair
Was good to see you lying there
We woke and saw the day arise
Tired feet and weary eyes
I'll walk with you each day until
My longing heart is calm and still
Dressing up to face the cold
This ritual will not grow old

You and I, in my dream
Gentle footsteps by the stream
Icy days and warming touch
We never felt this way so much
This I dream most every night
Of how I held your hand so tight
How we kissed, I loved those days
Strange this life and how it plays
These dreams of you will never go
The love I have, you'll never know
These walks in winter in my head
I lay alone in my bed
The fantasy of you and I
Enough to make a grown man cry
Tomorrow dawns and I am here
And in my dream, you were so near
Alone I face another day
I grab my coat and walk away.

Chalk

Let's take a walk
Let's talk
Let's draw a line
Let's use chalk.

Tick Tock

Tick tock.. life changes
Faces grow, life rearranges
I stood my ground on different stages
To get this far has taken ages.
Tick tock, the clock is counting down
I will not shudder,
I'll stand my ground
Hear the sound.
Tick tock again, the beating heart
Where did it end?
Where do we start?
Apart?
Apart is where we began.
Full circle now, I flee, I ran.
Tick tock, time passes by alone
I held my own
I tried. I cried.
I don't know why the clock still chimes
I'll never stop to write these lines.
Tick tock, the minutes pass so fast.
Will this time fade, or will it last?

Choices

Rainbows fade as the rain goes away
Like hope disappears at the end of the day.
A candles light, goes in a breath
The darkness comes when there's no light left.
Forgiveness is there once hearts have broken
A soul that's lost is found when woken
Moments change, a truth is told
Life flickers brief, once young, now old.
And in an instant, once that was
No longer shines, because
A butterfly once spread its wings
And changed the course of all these things.
Moments flicker, decisions change
Adapt, adjust, and rearrange
See each moment that you take
Observe the changes that you make
So, in a moment, stop and see
The changes that you made in me
Faith can fade as storms subside
Hope will shine, I'll take this ride
My candle's light will never fade
These are the choices that I've made.

The Common Road

We could take the road less travelled
We would fall along the way
The brambles and the untread path
Would make us weave and stray
We could have taken the common road
And be just like the rest
We'd play the game
Lived life the same
But would it be the best?
We could take the road less travelled
We could fight until the end
The brambles cut; the path trod down
What message would that send?
We didn't take the common road
And like so few, we fell
We played the game
Lived life the same
But was it worth the hell?
I now can see a new road
You're there, but not in breath
The brambles cut but do not hold
What part of me is left?
We stood beside the common road
We watched the passers by
And every time
We saw the signs
I held your hand and cried.

Cry

This tear on my cheek is for so many things
For the love that I lost, the beauty it brings.
The success of another, the loss of a friend
The closeness of strangers
A heart on the mend
This tear on my face is making me cry
Where does it go to? Why do I try?
This tear on my cheek is for so many years
Of wasting a life
Crying these tears.
Let's make this real...
So, tell me how you feel
World abused, destroyed, confused
Feelings hurt; my mind infused
With pain and punishment
Torment, torture
See my heart, see my future
Take my hand or take a bow
This is who I am right now
Take your issues, move aside
You never know how I feel inside
And now this pain you inject in me
Will never be the end of me
'Cause I will fight to bitter end
I will not accept the pain you send.
Take a bow, move aside
You'll never know how I feel inside.

Your show is over
You lost the war
I'll never see you again how I saw you before
Your show is over
I won the fight
And you won't see me smile tonight.
It hurts
The pain
Of never seeing you again.
But the energy you took from me
Will be the pulse that sets me free
Take a bow and go your way
I've had enough of you today
Life goes on without you
Pain still fades without you
Take my chances, play the game
Life will never be the same
I hate you more now you're not here
I love you more, let's make that clear
Fighting, biting, holding near
Doubting you
My greatest fear.
Your show is over
You lost the war
I'll never see you again how I saw you before
Your show is over
I won the fight
And you won't see me smile tonight.

Nobody Cared

The truth is nobody cares.
I said it. There it is.
Nobody gives a care.
Unless you stood up and made a stand
When that person needed you there.
If you hide your feelings and
Closed the door
Don't expect the door to open
When you need them more.
Shine before the door gets closed.
Proclaim before the sunset dawns
Be the person your heart is calling
Be there for those when they are falling.
Knock the door. Insist your love.
And by the grace of God above
They will respond.
They will wake up.
They will not holler or shut up.
Comfort comes in many forms
To some a touch is enough
To others a conversation is too rough
A hand. A smile is all it takes
To shake the negative. Awake.
Wake up to a brand-new day
The truth is out here, so they say.
What is the truth?
How should I feel?

Is this melancholy so real?
The truth is you are on your own
Laptop, job, mobile phone.
But what inside is making noise?
Stamping feet of girls and boys.
Making noise to change the future
Someone cried?
I can't remember.
The truth is that you're on your own
Fight
Live
Trust
Love
And most of all…
Never remember (regret).

Echoes

Echoes of history darken every street
Our minds and vision filled with terror
Life enlightens all those we meet
Personally, on TV screens,
In victory and defeat
Dreams of futures torn apart
Stories told to break every heart
Helplessly we watch the storm
History was there to warn
We stood and waited
Breath baited
And now reality hits hard
Should we turn every card?
Broken bones and broken lives
Sticks and stones, bombs, and knives
Shelter, run, stay and fight
Where will we be tomorrow night?
In distant lands we watch and pray
That someone, somewhere will end this
That someone, somewhere will be our hero
Stop this
Help us
Be here now, not tomorrow
And on these TV screens we see
A desperate and anguished nation
Every channel, every station
Where did this world go so wrong?

Who sent us to this damnation?
Where is the relation to this and what we knew?
Stable turned to fracture, yellow and the blue.
Sunlight blazes through cracked walls
Empty schools and empty halls
Litter strewn on every street
Scared of those who pass us
Frightened of the men we meet.
Take us to a better dawn and shelter us
Show us the future that we dreamed of
The road beneath our feet, untarnished by war
Show us who we are
Hold us, be us, breathe the air we miss
And in this nightmare, let dreams awake
Tomorrow will be our future.
Take this as our past and may this torment never last.
We stood and waited. Bated breath
We waited 'till there's nothing left.

Train Departed.

No queue at the station
The train departed
Not a mention
Litter blows across the platform
Stood alone
What did I fight for?
Baggage lays beside me
Inside the loss of how you left me
Tannoy silent
No more train
Memories of you again
Sad, dejected, feeling numb
Will the next train ever come?
No queue at the station
Not a soul upon the platform
No one here, no one near.
Tannoy silent
Silent fear
I'm left alone
I'm standing here.

The shyness of a longing heart, Part 1.

I miss you even though
You never would have known
I crave the hugs we've never had
But dream of when alone
I see your beauty shining
In everything I view
Each waking hour, each sleepless night
The vision is of you
I missed you tonight
And you are unaware
That I sit alone and dream your smile
I look, but you're not there.

Father's Prayer

One last cup of tea
Before we take our things and leave
One more cuddle on the way
Before we say goodbye today.
I'll put you on a train.
I may never see you again.
I'll pray that every night I stand
That one day soon
I'll hold your hand
And we will make a cup of tea
And cuddle close, you and me.

Today

Today was a bad day,
Though no different, not the best
Today I felt more broken
More painful than the rest.
Today was such a struggle
No hope was in my sight
Today I felt more vulnerable
I didn't feel quite right.
Today I had a wobble
My emotions ran amok
Today I felt like giving up
I wanted it to stop
Today was just another day
My heart took charge and won
Today is now behind me
Tomorrow has begun
So today will be a different script
Today I'll take a stand
And be the man I'm meant to be
Today is in my hands
And this will be my finest hour
Today I start anew
I start today with open eyes
And all because of you.
Today you made me stronger
More vibrant and alive
Today I face the world again

I'll more than just survive
Tomorrow's looking promising
Tomorrow they will see
That yesterday was just a blip
Today is meant for me.

We Made It Together

Gazing from a mountain
Where everything is empty
Standing lonely, looking out
And time is irrelevant
Silence fills my lungs
Breath is full and giving
Vision blurs endlessly
Yet nature fills my eyes
Hopeless futures come
The greyness fills the skies
Damp as sodden grass
Beneath my aging feet
I've trodden down these hills before
I've walked this dead-end street
Reality hits hard
I've grown and I have wandered
My life before me on this tump
The memories I've squandered
Sit. Let's talk.
I have memories to share
Of giants, witches, photographs

Of when I didn't care.
So, leap with me, off this hill
Go rolling in the grass
Tonight, we dream of all the smells
The life we live so fast
Take my hand, we'll go together
1.2.3 Jump.
We made it. You and I
We made it together
Even though you are no longer here.

We Never Shared A Past

We never shared a past
We never saw the future
I stood beside the lonely road
And gazed on what was greater.
I prayed for tomorrow
But tomorrow never came
And every day I live this life
This life still feels the same.
Every tune within my heart
Plays constantly anew.
If you held my hand tonight
I saw you shining through.
We never shared a future
We never saw the past
I stood beside a busy road
This life will never last.
Despite the heart, regret the fear
A moment in my soul
Take a look at all we know
Gaze upon my all.

See The Future Bright.

Stranded in the depths of time
We held on to unhindered truths
Laid our souls on the line of faith
Gave everything to a future
Beyond the walls of lies
We gazed on what we saw behind.
What we were born to believe as we grew.
Yet, in my heart, in my deepest memory
I recall a brighter future; something new.
A life on unforgiving joy
Where happiness and wrought emotion
Made me a man, before I knew.
They laid bare a universe of opportunity.
Here, now, a struggle for breath.
Today sees clouds draw closer, nothing left.
Looming shadows hover over a life I once imagined.
Where does the sunshine begin?
Alone again
I face the world each day with a mere grin.
Stand up. Embrace the dark, see the win.
The soaring eagle,
Graceful lark.
Change the script beyond the deepest part.
I'll stand with you
Or I'll stand alone.
Believe the sunshine of tomorrow
I am me.
I am home.

I Took My Heart Home

Didn't want to play today
Picked up my ball and stepped outside
Nothing seemed to go my way
I did my best. I did. I tried.
The bigger boys were mean today
They don't know how I tick
Nothing ever goes my way
I can't go on; it makes me sick
I never want to play again
Not by the rules that others make
Their rules are driving me insane
I've used the chances I could take
I'll take my ball and run-on home
I'll hide it somewhere no one can see
I'm better off just on my own
I'm better off just being me
I took my ball, my hate and fear
Hidden now until I'm set
To show the world again I'm here
Until then, let's just forget.

Say Something, Please.

Somehow, you're in my dreams
But I never gave you the key
And every night you wander in
You stand in front of me.
Your face is there
Your body too
And in my dream, we talk a lot
And I'm in love with you.
I see you and you're wonderful
You're everything I need
You're beautiful, you're gracious.
You make my soul seem freed.
Say something, please.

The Same Boat

Your skin's a different colour
You think differently to me
A homosexual, an amputee
A man, woman or even child
Life indoors or in the wild.
Christian, Raver, Buddhist
Rich man, poor man, or drama queen
Wake up, see what's unseen.
Suffering or doing well

Close your eyes, who can tell?
Freckles, directors, homeless, old
Grey, red, blonde, brunette
Student, master, and cadet
We all inhabit this one space
Our hearts inhabit the same place
One common ground, one faithful soul
Your heart stays true
Share your journey, just be you
Embrace those who enter in
Human faith, so let's begin...

Generation

The characterisation of this nation
Will be defined by those on PlayStation
By those who YouTube, TikTok and Instagram
They look to Greta for inspiration
Whilst guzzling power from power stations
To fuel the need for popularity
Images, duck faces, shoot yourself in jealous places
Rank the way to hashtag number one
Technology; the new engineer
Pleased to meet you, you're not here
A glitch of pixels in people's places
Faces, races, hearts, and aces
Are you grime? Trap? What new genre are we
spewing?
It's our undoing. To think we never had this crap.
We started it, though, didn't we?
Free love, Spectrums, camera phone.
No one wants to feel alone.
Connected through the web of the world
To every nation.
All fighting to be the next one, the best one.
Viral heroes and villains play their part
The next sensation.
And English, maths and science go by the wayside
When millions are made from a blindside
We never saw coming
And the humming of the power station
Grows as Greta speaks to the nation

The planet dies, electrification
The message broadcast for all to see
On electric powered devices of plastic
Fantastic. Why did we not see?
This generation, this nation, they know the way
Even if it is through play
Do we put our trust in these grime fed kids?
Their Fortnite battles, online vids?
I think we'll pass the baton on, despite the song
Give them the chance to make it right
They seem to know
Are they wrong, awake at night
Thinking of how a new world order could arise
From Playstations, Hip-Hop, TikTok and memes?
Who knows?
Humanity grows. Humanity flows and humans go
Where no human has gone before
So be sure
The future now lies in those we raise
Our days are numbered. Blundered.
Trust them, let them go unto the world
Let this new generation thrust themselves
Into a landscape of peril
Fix it, mix it, grime and Brexit
Virus, planet, show me the exit
This much is true, you PlayStation generation
Take this nation, this world, and make it you.

Grey & Distant Future

In the grey and distant future
Clouds cave in and swallow my hope
Sunshine hides behind beliefs
Brighter days retract to where love dies
Look further - to lightened skies
Where hope and faith re-grow
Breathe this sigh of relief
Take my soul and wrap in tight
We may be broken.. but tonight
I feel alright.
A grey and distant future
Spreads shadows where angels fall
I 've been there, trust me
I saw the rise; I am the fall.
In the bright and near future
Clouds are braking, sunshine powers through
I saw you.

Refugee

We ran, we cried, we took our freedom
Then we died.
We thought this was the way we were
We lived our life
We saw our life so planed out
Sure, we saw the danger
A foreign stranger
Bombs
Close and in our faces
Moving us from here to places
Is it our race
Or just our faces?
Take us home
Wherever that belongs
Unaware or western songs
Unashamed of how we look
Denied of education book
Female
Forgotten
Up for fun
Show me where I need to run
I run to where I need to hide
You'll never see the fear inside
I ran. I cried.
He died.
Save me please, I beg you now
Give me the freedom I crave inside.

Don't Worry About Me

I thought I'd lost my mind
Wanted to leave this life behind
Grab the reigns and steer toward the horizon
Just me, on my own
See what surprising road muted the pain
Never to be seen again
I thought the world would never miss me
No one would ever want to kiss me
I cried once too many times
Before I realised
Time can heal the hurt inside.
Deepest pain of solitude
Cuts harder than the pain of losing you
Anger contained in emotional wrath
Songs of yesterday hold me back
Let me step into tomorrow's winter sun
To see how life is now.
It's OK. It's fine.
Saddle up.
Don't let me trouble you with my mind.
It's fine.
Just let me live this new life of mine.

To Those

To those who held me close
To those who shared my pain
I needed all the love you gave
(I might need it again)
To those who tried to comfort me
To those I turned away
Keep going with your compassion
(I'll need you too someday)
And if you find you're in my place
And find you feel the fear
Be rest assured, I'll share your pain
(You'll forever find me here)

We danced

We danced, didn't we?
We saw the same future
We saw the light and danced all night
The future getting brighter.
We grew, didn't we?
We made our future.
We loved and cried, despite ourselves
Made life a little lighter.
We knew, didn't we?
We saw the end way too soon

And both of us were fighters
But lose, didn't we?
We knew the path was darker
And so, we ran, in different ways
Tomorrow to a stranger
Tears of sadness
Tears of pain
Never feel this way again
Until tomorrow I will shy
From this life that passes by.
We danced. We loved, until the end.
This broken heart will never mend.
We danced, didn't we?
Tell me it wasn't for nothing.
I must hold on
Despite it all
I must dream of something.

Solitude Hurts

My silent thought: my soul it shakes
My body rests, my mind awakes
My heart it beats, it feels the pain
Of never feeling you again.
I danced tonight
I won't again.
Darkest shadows, light remains.
My mind it reels of how we met
I lie here silent, not done yet
I take my chance; I go out loud
The loneliness has done me proud
I cried again.
A lonely cloud.
Lighter shades, my heart allowed.
Take my heart, my only vow
My breath belongs to you right now
My mind it wanders through the haze
And counting down these lonely days
I danced tonight.
I will again
Take my hand, my only friend.

Dancing in Rainbows

Sunshine doesn't need a rainbow
Light is loudest in the dark
A love can end when eyes are closed
Yet ignited by a moment's spark
Truths are told in abundance
But ears are blinded by the lies
We see the pain and feel the wonder
Turn our gaze to these blue skies
Search for freedom in the daylight
At night we pause and seek the lost
Join the crowd and be the player
Or stand alone at any cost
Nature comes to rival nurture
A conflict of our childhood dreams
Fortune over gracious favour
Is this journey all it seems?
Remind me of who I am tonight
Send me images and plays
Of how the future seemed so bright
How we'd prevail these storm bled days
Choices lead to reck or ruin
If taken by the self alone
Rainbows, sunshine, and the rain
This beauty shows us how we've grown
And now I dream of these rainbows
Poets aid their sad romance
Take the dreams, see the sunshine
Stand out in the rain and dance.

Life On A Page

I'm tired all the time, but I wanted to see
This future of mine and who I could be
So, I ran through the night, and I played with the
fire
I held on too tight, and I trusted a liar
I looked for the angels in bars and in solitude
A tempted young heart, beckoning fortitude
As time passes by and I watch it take hold
I cannot escape this race when I'm old
So I'll take all the chances of just being me
The others can watch, they just cannot see
The fire: it burns. It comes back to haunt
These phantoms of youth still hurt when they
taunt
I wanted to trust just how it would be
My life on a page that I no longer see.

Here We Stand

Here we stand
Or here we fall
When did we accept this all?
Our life before us torn to shreds
Our empty minds
Our empty heads.
Open our hearts to find
The life we seem
To love behind.
And so my soul
My heart I give
Upon this cross
My life I give.
The final breath
This sacrifice
Now I can live this life so right.
Our sin, your sacrifice so pure
Your death for me so sure
God help you bring my soul to pray
Another sunset
Another day
Bring me to this life so true
Another me,
Because of you.

My Sofa

My sofa isn't made for two
It's smaller than a pygmy's shoe
So, if you want to watch T.V
You'll have to sit upon my knee.
Or the floor
The floor's ok
I vacuumed it.
Sit.

Bought a half bottle.

Bought a half bottle of gin
I'm already about halfway in
When did this loop begin?
Feels so good, I know it's sin.
Mixed it with a splash of tonic
Now my words are less than phonic
The morning pain will be so chronic
My truth has turned out so ironic
Take each day and make it shine
Leave the dusk and past behind
Sit down and write the words that rhyme
Contemplate this life of mine.
Bought a half-life full of lies
So why is this as no surprise

This liquid comfort blurs my eyes
And keeps my focus off the prize.
Tomorrow's dawn, I'll start anew
This feeling, deep, of something true
A reborn hope, shining through
No painful truth of me and you.
A new horizon, target set
But wait a while, we're not there yet
There's still a past we must forget
Leave it behind with no regret.
New adventures waiting near
A future that I long to hear
So screw the gin and ditch the beer
My future now must be so clear
But now, tonight, the drink is gone
I listen to the saddest song
I rest my head, tonight was wrong
My future's here, it won't be long.
Bought a half-life, gave it away
For happiness again some day
Bought a half bottle of gin
Let this new chapter begin.

Be today

My confidence is fragile, what I trust is in a
spider's web
I tread the boards of this lonely stage
My wish for somewhere else instead
Sadness comes, it ebbs and flows
It weaves its fear and dread
Angels see and take my heart
Breathe life when I was dead
My second chance is precious, what I trust is true
Fragility of life's embrace
Begins with me and You
Glory comes, it raises hope
Words we always knew
Angels see and hold my hand
To make this my debut
Raise your voice and shine your light, what you
trust is good
Walk the line with outright faith
Be who you know you should
Redemption comes, it blazes bright
No shadows where you stood
Live for now, tomorrow's child
Be heard. Be understood.

Captain Sir

Grace and fortitude prevailed
Upon your golden wings we sailed
Our mettle tested, we ingested
Sentiment: it never failed.
You did not take the seat rear row
Soldier, singer, social hero
Walked, inspired, and taught us grace
So let us not return to zero.
And while we watched his valiant stride
We tried our best and stayed inside
Here stood a giant, yet so mild
Deep within our national pride
Walk on, you military saint
The irony, it shall not taint
Our image of you; smiling
Without a grumble or complaint
Sir Tom, a legend, man, inspires
As we walk through unknown fires
Walk again, my inspiration
The whole world stands, the world admires.

Stages of Parental Love

Shut up. You're screaming. You're too much in
my face.
Get out. You're evil. You dominate this place.
I love you. You're wonderful. I adore your lively
play.
And how you cuddle, snuggle me, has made me
feel this way.
Shut up. Sit down. Do what you're told.
Don't play that game, your food is cold.
You are the best, you're clever. Your work is so
sublime.
I'm proud of what you have achieved, my brilliant
son of mine.
I'll take away your Xbox, your PC and your phone
Get out, get off, just leave me. I need to think
alone.
So, cuddles now are awesome, you snuggle up
so well
Your peaceful face, angelic look, you've got me
in your spell.
I have to turn the network off; you play that game
too late
You make my blood boil, make me tense, make
me scream, but wait..
You are a human, just like me. Your passion
makes me think.

That you are right, and I am wrong, my logic on
the brink..
If this digital display makes you happy today
Then play my son, play on
Who am I to judge your choice?
Play on, my son, play on.
Look at me, I am not much, I yell at from my past
Has that not got me to a place where happiness
that lasts?
Shout, holler, do your best, be who you want to
be.
Don't follow in my footsteps, be you. Be strong. Be
free.
And though you test my patience, you clever son
of mine
Your character and strength of will, will help me
leave behind
The anger of a lockdown day when we're both
head-to-head.
So, cuddle me, my loving child, just think of what I
said.
The future's yours so take it, rise up and take the
prize
Give your thanks to Lord our God and be glad to
be alive
Together we will make it, so hug me; set me free.
The future is there waiting, be yourself, and don't
be me.

Walking Through Mud.

Images of past treks
Lowly spirits and cold boots
Raised by mother nature's bliss
This muddy, river carved pathway
Upwards. Paving the way
To a greener, flatter landscape
Made it all worthwhile
Sticky boots for half a mile
Biting breeze on kept-in faces
Monuments. Historical places
Dogs are wild, roaming in the woods
Playing ball on fields we seldom tread
Who said a walk wouldn't do us good?
Scenery of cities and silence
Unblinded by the tech behind us
Biting breeze upon our cheeks
A freshness we have not felt for weeks
Sticks and twigs, crackle under foot
Silence broken by song of spring
Wrapped up warm and unafraid
Of new adventures today we made
Explorers of this land so near
We feel at one; and here
Beneath our feet where we seldom tread
Is life worth living
So give us this day, our daily bread
Fresh baked and filling our nostrils

With life's better moments.
Wake up, walk up this river carved pathway
Maybe today, you too will say
Nature brings the biting bliss
No better feeling than this.
Crisp and open
Wild and free
Sticks and stones
You and me.

As Children Do

Playing games as children when parents were
away
Climbing on the haystacks, you and me.
My fantasy of you as gorgeous as you were
As beautiful as you are.
Tomorrow when I wake
I will not fear the sounds or sights
Of those who saw
Of those who have never seen
Those who never had the love we had
Find the journey
Discover and find the path we took
To those who never travelled, look…
I look into your eyes and pray
That you and I will be one
Despite our thoughts on east and west
Society would never know
Hold my soul, hold my heart
Our love aligns so beautiful
We do not see the pain
We see us, together.

If, Again

If your sunset fades.
If tomorrow shrinks into the shade
If the future seems far away
If today was hard to play
If today was hard to grasp
Then bless you friend, it will not last.
If you wake and feel alone
If you step on jagged stones
If you fall and feel the pain
Then stand up proud and walk again
If you wake and face the day
With a smile and hope and pray
Then you will be a better man
And i will love you as I can.
If you can say you stayed at home
Despite the feeling of alone
If you can say you played your part
You gave it all, all your heart
Then stand before me, as if you care.
If I love you, I'll be there.

Where We Tread

Preliminary steps shall not define
Paths we choose to leave behind.
Footprints in the melting snow
Will never show the way we go.
Glance over shoulder at the track
Memories show no way back
Decisions made, the unknown paved
No way to change how we behaved
Regrets, a few, but that's our lot
If we should dwell, that's all we've got
Face the wind, tilt head down low
And walk towards what you don't know
How did this future come so fast?
Don't back now, don't see the past
Where foot and feeling define time
Look and see this life of mine
The shadows fade, the glimmer; bright
Darker days, a brighter night
As demons fade on darker walls
Past is fading, future calls
I'll plan and ponder when I wake
Clear elation righteous makes
Stand me on a mountain high
Play the song I learnt to cry
Point me forward, make me grow
Hide my footprints in the snow.

Yo-

-nder skies of fading red
-nder life, the day we met.
Finding yo- was so intense
Loving yo- was recompense
Yo- held my hand.
Yo- held my heart
Finding yo- was j-st the start.
We danced that night, We were alone
-nder skies of fading bl-e
I dreamed of -s,
Of me and yo-
Where are yo-
Where are yo- now
I miss yo-
Yo- are no longer here
I can not face the f-t-re
Witho-t y-o near.
Where are yo-?

Another Life

A dusty sunset/
Another life/
Another man/
Another wife/
A death/
A fall/
A steady rise/
A definite mean to all the lies/
A momentary lapse of reason/
Of truth/
Of fault/
Of sin/
Of treason/
A lasting body/
One long strife/
A dusty sunset/
Another life.

You're Unique

They said "don't show your ugly face"
They told you to behave
They told you not to make a noise
They said "don't make a wave"
Stay in your box
Confirm, obey.
Just do as you are told.
Say no to all the rules and regs.
(It's too late when you're old.)
Don't let the hateful grind you down.
Just shout out "this is me"
The freedom that you're gifted with
Should mean that you are free.
Condition can be changed.
Go back to who you were.
Celebrate your uniqueness
Be true, be you, be pure.
Believe in the truth of life
See who you'll become
By following your heart's desire
Let mind and faith be one
And in the darkness of your days
Have strength in your unique
Your intuition will shine through
The solace that you seek.
Be master of your destiny
Wake up each day and pray
That everything you stood for
Will see you good someday.

Under rainclouds

This illumination of our being
Wakes us up to this life we are seeing.
Transfixed by the media
Believe it if you will.
Staring skyward toward a future
Eyes ablaze, redundant in a frenzy of false truth
Stay true, believe
That everything you see is not verbatim
Under these rain clouds of lies
We search for sunshine in the skies
We wake each day and battle on
But something is wrong
Society predicates our future
I woke up again today
To a feeling of disparity
I seek a clarity
A lifetime tutor to teach
Deeper feelings than those who preach
So, the sky is where I stare
Looking to see if anything's there
Under rain clouds, standing true
The rain will fall
But so will you.

Printed in Great Britain
by Amazon

16524694R00050